CNY: Customer Awareness

Bobby Simonds

ISBN: 1974031535

ISBN 13: **9781974031535**

Library of Congress Control Number: **XXXXX**

LCCN Imprint Name: **City and State**

bobby.simonds@gmail.com

www.facebook.com/bobbyraysimonds

www.facebook.com/bobbyrsimonds

www.instagram.com/@bobbysimonds

#bobbyraysimonds

#bobbysimonds

#BOBBYRAYSIMONDS

#ATWISTINTRAVEL

#risenfromtheashes

#toxicamerica

#Challenge-thyself

#avoidinghavoc

I dedicate this short review book to those living in Central New York, who know that you can't count on the professionals for recommendations, but in reality, it all comes down to *real* people!

Preface

I will be sharing with you the facts with my experience with shopping & eating at various shops/restaurants in Central New York, that I have gone to.

This will be my customer experience, the pro's & con's of what I liked & didn't; just as many of us would imagine before entering a store!

McDonald's - Clinton

Everyone knows *McDonald's*. But what they don't know is what happens *behind the scenes*. I used to work for this location, and rarely return for a meal. Not because the price of food has all gone up. Especially with the intended $15 an hour increase - expected in 2017.

What happens behind the scene is extremely important, which is rarely told to the public. The *health department* is fully aware - whether they come forward or deny the truth.

The truth is simple. Workers walk by the "prep" table constantly thru a shift, and majority of them are the cashiers - majority of customers are annoyed with. The issue with the cashiers that walks past this prep table, is that they're not wearing gloves.

In fact, majority of employees at McDonald's (at least), is that most employees don't wash their hands when they should, and they stick their filthy hands (continuously) in the *Pickle* container. You know almost every lunch/dinner sandwich receives a pickle or two; and your eating these disgusting pickles everyone is sticking their hands in the container.

The other thing (at least when I worked at this store from 2006-2008), is that when the lettuce or tomato's start to go bad (or already is well past the expiration date) they still serve this food, because the store doesn't want to *eat the loss*!

I remember when I had worked there, I attempted to throw out the bad produce & was issued a *Verbal Warning!* This also happens with the buns & wraps.

When I worked here, they used a dirty trick

on customers. This trick was ever so simple. They ran the buns thru the *Bun-Warmer;* and with the wraps, they'd throw them on the grill for 1-minute.

I don't know if they still do this, and if others do this, but it wouldn't surprise me any if they did. After all, how many times has everyone (customers) been pissed off beyond recognition after going to any various fast food establishment, especially with McDonald's? Yet, humans continuously return, and face the same probability of receiving the wrong order, the screwed up order, or worse, food poisoning!

Hobby Lobby - New Hartford

There isn't anything bad about this place in my opinion. They have a great line of products and the people that work there are always knowledgeable and polite.

This store carries plenty of *fake* plants, arts & crafts, holiday decorations, and so much more. There prices can be high, but you just need to look for coupons online.

Dollar General - Waterville

The shelves are cramped, the people rude, the prices aren't *generally a dollar.* So why shop here? The convenience. That's about it.

Be aware, they're particularly rude when it's slow, and they watch many like a hawk, if you don't purchase anything!

From what I hear, it's not a good company to work for either. Some have told me, that working at McDonald's is way better, and in my opinion, that says a lot!

Dollar General - NY

Ironically, even though they carry the same products from NY to FL, the workers are way different, in every way!

People seem to be much more polite, easy going and happy in Florida. They don't care, one way or the other, if you purchase something or just want to browse.

The people in Upstate New York are generally grumpy to be around. There are few that are pleasant, but most are so nasty to even have to be within their presence!

Stewart's Gas Station - Waterville

The price is right! The *smoke's* are about average, sometimes a quarter higher depending on brand.

The coffee not only excellent, but the cheapest in comparison of everywhere! Recently found out that after 3 pm, coffee is between 30-50 percent off!

In 2016, they finally had added pizza to their menu. Overall, the price is more than fair. Majority of the time, you can receive attitude for ordering a pizza; but it isn't terrible. I can honestly say, it's better than some of the Pizza 'joints' I've had had in the county!

Majority of the time, the people are positively good, and others are moodier than they aught to be. Nonetheless, if you want a job here, make sure you know someone!

Nice-n-Easy - Sangerfield/Waterville

A decent place to get drinks, pizza, subs, and many other food items. They have dry stock as well - but expect to pay higher prices, in comparison of grocery stores. They do this to make it more convenient for the customer. I don't think their prices are reasonable, and the customer service is a hit and miss (even before I had worked there for a few months).

This company has the highest turn-over rate for employees I've ever seen. I believe it's due to the management. The store manager literally went from a *Shift Manager* to a Store Manager. They hire dumb people (majority of the time), and always receive the same outcome.

Their gas is reasonably priced, but for some

reason in the winter season, you get about half the mileage you would in the summer. It isn't the slow going speeds, it's just the way it is. The locals sometimes compare their gas with *Savon On*, which is the Indian owned gas stations in Oneida.

Burger King - New Hartford

Burger King is known for the Burgers & chicken. Both are good. Recently, with all the various food prices increasing, they have the 2 for $5 original chicken sandwich; or you can get the 1 double burger & a chicken sandwich; or you can do two of both (as long its only 1 of the 2 items). This includes small fries, tiny bacon cheeseburger, 4-piece chicken nugget and any drink from the menu.

My wife and I thoroughly enjoy the *Ice Coffee drinks* - which sounds really good right now! The only downsize is the one size only for these two flavors: Vanilla or Mocha - both very good; but my favorite is the Vanilla Ice Coffee mix. It's generally gone in less than five minutes because it's so well made.

The one major warning I must prep you for, however, is the Ice coffee's. Sometimes (not always), they hand the customer the same drink saying it's the opposite. This happened to my wife & I the other day. We ordered a Vanilla Ice Coffee (for me), and a Mocha Ice Coffee (for her). They handed us two Vanilla's saying that they were separate. My wife, went inside after we exited the *drive-thru*, and made them remake it until it was right (two more times)!

Taco Bell - New York Mills

Very few times have I gotten an order screwed up, let alone take forever. But I also know that if you want the order right & swift, don't go after 8 pm (any day of the week).

The company has brought a breakfast menu in to the mix - if you didn't know. And the prices are excellent, and so are the items.

My sister worked for the Taco Bell in Oneida, and she truly loved working there - for the most part.

The pay is the same as any other fast food joint; but they do offer benefits for all shifts, which most places, especially McDonald's doesn't offer; unless your in management.

Taco Bell/Long John Silvers - Oneida

The food is great, never had bad service; the same results and reviews as the one previously reviewed. (New York Mills). Enough said, moving on!

Walmart - New Hartford

If you haven't done your grocery shopping here, I feel sorry for you. This is the store to shop at!

I don't like what they represent, and I hate the fact that they force *the Ma' & Pop* stores to close all across our great nation. Nevertheless, they're priced right, and then some.

They have almost every type of product a human needs to survive. However, be aware, when you plan on purchasing one thing, you generally walk out with more than one item.

I've heard that they're like many various fast food joints. The pay sucks, the management just as bad. Nonetheless, it's even harder to get in for employment, if you're intelligent like myself. It seems that they hire a ton of parents & college students. They also seem to hire a lot of people on welfare programs. I've attempted to work there, but never got into the store for employment.

I truly believe that in comparison of every grocery store, they are the cheapest, and most items are the freshest as well. The beef and chicken are debatable, however. As far as produce goes, the best items to get are in the freezer, but the prices are very reasonable.

Another thing that you, as the customer, should be aware of. When shopping for pet food, toys, bedding, fish food, cat supplies, etc., you should start shopping here. They have the same products as other pet stores, only cheaper. You can even find cat litter for just over a dollar a bag (which is enough for two litter cleanings)!

Walmart - Utica & Oneida

The same results as the one above (New Hartford); only difference is the layout of the store is very different. These two locations make's things more difficult to locate (even in produce). The customers are more moody as well - so keep that in mind if you want to shop here for the holidays!

Best Buy - New Hartford

I've never met a dooshbag employee here, but I have met a few morons! Who hasn't right?

The prices are much higher considering the name of the store, but they have much to offer.

This isn't a store high on my list to become a repeat shopper. Especially when *Amazon.com* exists. Majority of items in Best Buy, as I had mentioned, aren't *the best buys*. You get less for your money at this store, but I've heard it's a good job to carry.

Best Buy - Syracuse (Destiny USA)

Same results as the New Hartford location, only the *sales associates* are foxes. They outwit the customer, whether you know everything about a product or not. You are easily manipulated into purchasing extra accessories you weren't intending to purchase. Nevertheless, at least they know what they're doing, as they should!

Dollar Tree - New Hartford & Hamilton

Both store locations are about the same. The employees are courteous and welcoming. This store literally is a dollar for any item. People can get carried away with purchases here, as the store owners are fully aware.

"It's only a dollar, I may as well grab two!" I've heard that being said throughout the store from time to time, from random customers.

I worked for the New Hartford location for only a few weeks. It seemed good at first, but everyone was a conniving S.O.B. hoping that the store manager & other various managers would get fired, because the regular associates weren't being treated fairly. I worked with both the store manager and others, and I knew right off the bat, that the store manager deserved his position, and the "little guy/girl" didn't get promotions, due to punctuality issues and laziness. I didn't last because I couldn't stand the constant negativity and the lack of training from the Assistant Manager, who complained about everything & everyone (2014). It's a shame, but that's about how many retail companies are.

Hannafords - Clinton & New Hartford

Both locations are equally the same. This company has almost everything a grocery store should have on its shelves. However, they seem a bit pricey for a grocery store, when many times they don't have too many sales, and often times, I've had bad meat from their all too often.

I did hear that they're an excellent paying company to work for. But they've never hired me in the last 8 attempts; so I wouldn't know first hand!

Price Chopper - Hamilton, New Hartford, Utica

I've shopped at all three locations. However, my first choice is Hamilton. They're much polite and willing to be courteous and prompt with every customers' needs. Whereas the other two locations would rather make you wait for long periods of time, or just straight-out ignore you.

Price Chopper is a good company to work for, but difficult to get into for employment. Another place that you seem to have to know another employee to get into.

Target - New Hartford

I love this store, but they have become quite expensive in the past few years. Thanks to the recession (the first one), they've increased their prices by at least twenty percent.

I heard they are a great place to work, but haven't had any luck to get into employment.

Majority of the employees are cheerful and seem to be great at getting others to be outgoing. They have had some quiet college students working for them. They seem to always have a ton of college students working for them, and they seem to encourage that. So keep that in mind, and don't get to close to the student employees, because chances are, they're imported from other states!

Barnes & Nobles - New Hartford

I can't say much about this store, I have my books on selling on their web page!

What I can say, is that I love their WI-FI connection, it's the best in the county! Always a strong signal, but when the store is busy, it's difficult to connect.

The people are great. Always happy & helpful. My only true complaint, is that if you can sell books on their web page, they should at least have two paperback copies within the store. You never know if what a customer will purchase, yal' are unpredictable!

Rio Grande Tex Mex Grill - New Hartford

A bit pricy, but excellent food! The service hasn't ever let me down, and the spice is just right. I'd highly recommend this eatery! It's difficult to locate a good Mexican restaurant in this state!

Pedro's Kitchen - New Hartford

I highly recommend this restaurant. They always have good service, and excellent food. It's mostly a quiet, yet, Mexican decor. The salsa is great with the chips before the meal. The coffee could use some work, but most Mexicans I've met, don't usually drink coffee - not all but some.

This restaurant is family operated, and is located near 5 Guys.

5 Guys - New Hartford

A great place to work, and an even better place to eat!

The food is always cooked just right, the soft drinks always tasty.

I don't have anything bad to say about them, which is saying a lot!

Applebee's - New Hartford & Utica

I've visited both locations. Utica isn't nearly as good, but in recent years, I found that Applebee's continues to raise their prices dramatically after every menu change.

I've heard they're an *okay* company to work for. Their pay is average considering the high prices of their menu items.

My favorite thing on the menu is their alcohol beverages. Tasty and made properly - just as mix drinks should be. Most of us New Yorkers are mainly beer drinkers, but there seems to be an increase in mixed beverages - at last!

T.J. Max - New Hartford

If you've ever been to *Mervin's* or *Ross*, T.J. Max is no different. They're layout is identical, cramped clothing departments, nick-knacks, bathroom decor, towels, and other miscellaneous items, this store is very cramped, and in my opinion, disorganized. I'm not a big fan of this store.

My wife's first job was working for T.J. Max in California, and I've got to say, it hasn't changed much in the past twenty years, and three thousand miles apart (CA to NY); it's identical.

I heard they're a little bit better to work for here, but retail is retail. The pay sucks, and the management isn't any better. You get what you pay for...right?

Bed, Bath & Beyond - New Hartford

I absolutely love this store. However, they're a bit expensive. The people are genuine, and mostly helpful. If you have a *California King* mattress, like I do, you know it's nearly impossible to find sheets or blankets to fit it. They don't exactly supply that size in NY; therefore, this is the place to shop for linens, blankets & even excellent assortment of pillows.

They have many products, that I wish I had in my home. It's too over priced for my budget; but my mother shops there all the time.

I heard it's a great company to work for, but its a must to know what you're talking about, that way you don't look like a person whose never purchased anything you're selling!

Bass Pro Shop - Utica

This is one of my favorite stores. Not because it has all the fishing accessories or equipment one fishermen would need, but because it's a great place for clothing.

I found out that not every state carries the same type & quality of clothing as California had, when we used to live there (final year was 2006). In fact, considering the NY designers (in NY City), we get the crappy clothes, or *"Oh, that's so last year,"* clothing lines.

When Bass Pro Shop had finally come to Upstate New York, I was thrilled, because cargo pants are difficult to find. They're a little pricy, mainly because they are all *named-branded*; but it's worth the money if you can afford them.

I found that men clothing has been down-graded over the past decade. Perhaps it's because I have gotten older, and my taste in clothing has changed dramatically. Nevertheless, I truly love cargo-pants, because they never shrink, and they don't make your legs itch (due to the dye's in clothing). I haven't been unhappy with the clothes from this store. I highly recommend you to start shopping here for your men (for you woman), and visa verse. Because the female's clothing is just as good.

The best time to go shopping at this particular store is during a holiday weekend sale, because they really do stick with sales pricing. For example, most cargo pants are priced between $40-$80 (depending on brand). During the sales times mentioned, you can save between ten & thirty (also depending on brand). And they last a long time.

The pair I had bought back in May 2016, hasn't shrunk, hasn't stretched, hasn't stained (mostly), hasn't torn, and best of all, the color hasn't faded - like majority of clothes nowadays.

I've also heard that this store is one of the best stores to work at as far as retail goes. Everyone is always knowledgeable in their departments, they're always cheerful & sometimes even, overly happy. That is most certainly a good thing! Keep up the good work *Bass Pro Shop: owners, managers, & grunts!*

Pets Supply Plus - New Hartford

I enjoy browsing in this store, the products are basically the same as other pet products stores. The only difference is their rodents, birds & even fish departments. They do offer an array of rodents, including Ferrets & bunnies. With birds, they have sometimes had exotics; and with fish they've had the *cooler* looking fresh water. They even have a small section of *salt water fish, coral, star fish, & Nemo-styled* fish. Therefore, if you're into that sort of thing, you should come to this store!

Petsmart - New Hartford

Most people are friendly & curteous. However, the management tends to run & hide when seeing customers, or they'd prefer to stand around and talk.

Most people are inexperienced with pet-related products, and they tend to manipulate the customer into thinking they know (the worker) more than the customer.

Majority of the workers only work their, because they had a great idea, "I love animals." But they forget how much work is involved, which brings me to another point, they sometimes have a *high turnover rate.* Sometimes it isn't due to the pets, or the hard work, it can be due to the management team for not being experienced enough in their *fields of expertise.*

My wife works here, and enjoys the customer relations, pets, and sales. She is one of the most knowledgeable employees, because she's worked for *Petsmart* for over a decade.

If you decided to work for this company, keep in mind that if you want to become a manager, you must be controllable, otherwise, don't expect much room for advancement!

As far as product information goes, they have pretty much everything; only, the prices are a little steep - even with discounts.

Tractor Supply - Hamilton & Utica

I love this store, especially for dog food. They're by far the cheapest to shop at, and the *Hamilton* location is extremely helpful in helping the customer choose what's best for their pet.

Most of their products are reasonably priced, and if you have horses, this is a great place to go for supplies, food, and even treats!

This store even has clothing, although, I haven't experienced purchasing the clothing, my stepfather has, and enjoys both pants & shirts. Even my mother enjoys their clothing.

The employees are well above satisfactory, knowledgeable, & even enjoyable to be around. Generally speaking, the cashiers are generally the shyest employees.

Khol's - New Hartford

My mother is a huge fan of this store. For me, it's about the same as *T.J. Max.* The products are better quality (than T.J. Max), but it's also kind of cramped in various departments.

The workers are mostly knowledgeable, and friendly. Holiday season sucks donkey balls, but they offer many sales, especially on Wednesday's.

J.C. Penny's - New Hartford

Another store I enjoy shopping at. They have a *Big & Tall's* section for male's clothing. They have a variety of shoes, clothing, & jewelery to chose from. Many women in our area enjoy the Salon. The salon offer's reserved & walk-in hair styles, and they're fairly inexpensive. My wife used to go here, until she learned to style her own hair.

I recommend shopping at this store, even with the busy holiday shopping seasons!

Macy's - New Hartford

What can I say, *It's Macy's!* They have a vast variety of wears, kitchen sets, and a whole lot more. They have friendly customer service, they're not pushy for sales, and they're honest. There isn't much more to say..

Toys-R-Us - New Hartford

I enjoy looking around with both my nephew & my wife. They are filled with stuff I don't need! Nevertheless, it's a great place to kill some time with a *little one*. The prices are about average - with children's stuff. They have an awesome section for video games, toys, and *toddler driving cars!*

Most employees are knowledgeable, but there seems to be a huge turnover rate. Therefore, don't get too close to your favorite worker, they may be gone the next time you visit!

Wicker Mill - New Hartford (Borderline Utica)

Wicker Mill is a unique store. If you are a collector with wicker products, this is the store for you! I enjoy wicker myself, but they're products are priced to high for me. The people are friendly & knowledgeable.

Adirondack Furniture - Utica

An overpriced store filled with excellent hand-crafted, wood furniture. They do often furniture that isn't wood crafted, but everything in this store isn't meant for *the little guy...* Most sets are well over two thousand dollars, on the cheap side. Nonetheless, they do have excellent furniture, with great warranties, to boot. So if you're an *Upper Class-man*, you may want to check out their stuff!

FYE - New Hartford

A great place to go for both new & used music, movies, television shows, and other products. They offer a *membership, discount card*, but beware it's a total pain in the butt, when you want to cancel!

Everyone is genuine, and even knowledgeable. When you go to cash out, they often point out that they have sales, and push you into taking advantage. Beware of that part...sometimes you can save money, and other times it doesn't seem like much of a sale...

Boscovs - New Hartford

It took forever to open after *Sear's* had gone under. It was well worth the wait!

A store similar to *Macy's, J.C. Penny's, & Sear's* combination. The prices are well below than average, and they often have sales. Everyone has duly enjoyed shopping at this store after their grand-opening in October 2016. It hasn't slowed down any, the shopping has increased, due to the holiday shopping season. A great place to shop, for the money!

The appearance of the store is more than good. Everything is easy to find, one can easily get stranded in this store (if you are expected to *shop til you drop*). Even the employees seem thrilled to work there, even with dressing up. *Dress to impress*, seems to be their motto. It's good though, they even have a small amphitheater for entertainment!

The only thing I wouldn't encourage for future purchases, is their cheaper Pot's & Pans sets. They're dirt cheap for a reason. They tend to rust even though they claim their resistant to rust.

Babe's Bar & Grille - Utica

My wife & I love their food & drinks. They are about the only Restaurant that knows how to create a *Blue Hawaiian* alcohol beverage. And it's more than splendid!

The food is great, just expect paying at least ten dollars a meal (per person). The service is swift, friendly, & curious. They also don't take their time when you're ready to pay the bill and leave. A Grille that is worth checking out, that doesn't get a ton of referrals.

Denny's - New Hartford, Utica, & Oneida

A great place to eat. They changed the style of coffee, so if you enjoy drinking diesel fuel, then you'd love the coffee!

The food is constantly changing ever year, which means the prices of the food is continuously altered. All their varieties of food is always cooked with care & precision. They are way different than they used to be - I suppose they learned from the many lawsuits they used to get throughout the country!

Zebb's Deluxe Grill & Bar - New Hartford (they have one in Syracuse too)

We love eating here, the food is excellent, and the service is generally responsive. The best time to go is during the busy hours, that way you know there's no time for a break from the staff!

There was only two times we weren't satisfied, and majority of the time they don't give you discounts for complaints.

In any case, this is one of our favorite eateries, and I do highly suggest trying the *California Burger!* Very good burgers, one of my favorite restaurant-burger joints!

Gander Mountain - New Hartford

A great place to shop for clothing, weapons, hunting gear, and even shoes! The workers are always courteous & helpful. They only hire out-going people, which makes it a great place to experience every shopping need with these departments. They don't frown on the *looky-loo's* either.

Advance Auto - Utica, New Hartford, Hamilton

A sister company of Auto Zone; same products, same layout, same coloration of name/logo's.

People are always helpful; often generally friendly & experienced. Prices are generally averaged.

Auto Zone - New Hartford & Utica

Same as *Advanced Auto stores*. Read review previously, identical experience.

Pep Boys - New Hartford

A great place for minor repairs, tires, and miscellaneous accessories. The people are almost always helpful & friendly. The downfall is the waiting time.

This company needs more locations locally to help spread the business, and lower the waiting times.

If you decided to take your *rust-bucket* here, expect to be conned into expensive repairs. They love to encourage replacements on items you don't necessarily need, like *Goodyear (the reason why they probably closed in New Hartford)*. In addition, I wouldn't recommend going here for your annual *Inspection tag*, especially if you aren't driving a new vehicle.

Sangerfield Auto & Tire - Sangerfield/Waterville

The price is right, and the people are very knowledgeable. Descent tires for cheap, and this is the place to go for your *Inspection tags.* Fast service in comparison with other shops, and very helpful with return customers. Plus while you're waiting, the *Nice-n-Easy* store is literally across the road!

Dick's Sporting Goods - New Hartford

A bit over priced, but excellent quality clothing, sports goods, and even shoes. They even often warranties on shoes over $100.

They even often an excellent variety of winter clothes & snow pants. They're winter-line is probably the cheapest in comparison of other sporting goods stores.

The employees are knowledgeable, friendly, and not too pushy. A great place to shop, overall.

Herb Phllipson's - New Hartford, Oneida, Rome

This store is similar to *Dick's sporting goods,* the only difference, is the large variety of clothing, and they're cheaper, with the same brand names. The best time to shop here is late spring, early summer. They often offer a clearance rack, which in 2016, I was able to find great tank-tops for $5 each, with great quality.

They also have a great winter-gear line-up, and the prices are very reasonable. The people seem to love working here, because they're never moody, no matter how the customer may treat them!

Save a lot - New Hartford

This store is a lot like a grocery store. The prices are about average, sometimes less than. I wasn't really thrilled shopping here, because it seems *dumpy* to me. They don't seem to take much pride with appearance inside the store. But that doesn't mean they haven't updated since the last time I had gone (2012).

Aldi's - New Hartford, NY Mills & Canastoda

A ton of people, including myself, shop here. The prices are good, the people efficient. The produce is sometimes questionable - as the same can be said for the meat. Overall, this store is a good place to do your grocery shopping needs. You have to purchase or bring your own bags, and use a quarter for the use of a shopping cart. However, they do take pride in appearance within their store.

The best time to shop is when they first open, because they are constantly restocking their shelves due to the instant rushes they receive throughout the day.

Slaughtered Lamb - Waterville

A strange name for a bar & grille, but it does get your attention! I haven't had the pleasure eating or drinking here, but I've heard that they're excellent with both food quality & prompt service.

Being located in a small town, they have odd hours, so be weary of that. Another words, don't be surprised if they're closed - due to lack of customers!

I've often driven by, and have noticed they've been closed on Saturday's - which one wouldn't expect.

Another issue with this place, is that they close their business for their own days off, and they've only been in business a few years.

Morgan's Hardware - Waterville

This is a good place to shop locally when you need miscellaneous tools, gardening supplies, and plumbing. This is a family owned hardware store, and has been for years. There aren't many left. However, they're overpriced, and the furniture isn't worth your money. They are very knowledgeable, and very helpful with anything you may need to fix, that you need to be referred to purchase for your various fixing needs for your home.

If you do shop here, just keep in mind that most items you do expect to purchase, are marked higher, because they expect to charge more than the corporate-ran stores. It's the only way to survive - supposedly.

I don't shop there much, because you can get

everything in Waterville, and they don't support my books, so why should I support their store. I like shopping for the right price...I do shop there for my gardening tools, though.

Subway - Clinton & New Hartford

What can I say? Other than, I only eat one thing from them...Meatball Sub. It's almost always good, but the prices are too high for what you receive. People are good, and swift.

Once in awhile - usually after they open - they give you cold meatballs, be cautious with that.

In Closing:

It's clear to me, and you, that considering the small aspect of the area we live in, there's a ton of stores to choose from. My suggestion to you is, read up on these various stores if you want spectacular service!

Thanks for this purchase, and I hope that it had helped you in some way. Thanks again.

1) A twist in travel: Fate (sci-fi)

2) The incident of 12/6/14 (nonfiction)

3) A twist in travel: Scientific Wastelands (sci-fi)

4) J.J.'s Rhymin' Adventures: The Complete Series (kid's poetry)

5) The True Masterminds of Manipulation: Volume 1 (nonfiction)

6) The True Masterminds of Manipulation: Volume 2 (nonfiction)

7) The True Masterminds of Manipulation: Volume 3 (nonfiction)

8) Living with Mild Cerebral Palsy (bio)

9) The true masterminds of manipulation: The complete series (nonfiction)

10) An angry memo: attention all humans (nonfiction)

11) Mind boggling experiences of the weird & strange (nonfiction/paranormal)

12) Missing my dog, my best friend: Ginger (nonfiction/self-help)

13) Don't mind the little things! (nonfiction/self-help)

14) Where are all the good drivers? (nonfiction/self-help/educational)

15) Puggle fun with Ginger (picture book, young

children)

16) Do you have what it takes to become the next great author? (nonfiction/self-help/guidance/educational)

17) Family in Ruins: The loss from a suicide (nonfiction/self-help/guidance)

18) What is banned in America: Volume 1 (nonfiction/awareness)

19) Risen from the Ashes: Untold Truths & Theories (Volume 1; Political Awareness/nonfiction)

20) Empty Conversations: Dear Dad (nonfiction/grievance)

21) Risen from the Ashes: You be the judge (volume 2; nonfiction/political awareness)

22) Risen from the Ashes: Surrounded by Stupids (Volume 3; nonfiction/political awareness)

23) Risen from the Ashes: Living in an Unjust Society (Volume 4; nonfiction/political awareness)

24) A Twist in Travel: The End is Near (sci-fi/series)

25) A Twist in Travel: Trio (all 3 books; sci-fi/trilogy)

26) Risen from the Ashes: Broken Shackles, Part 1 (Volume 5; nonfiction/political awareness)

27) Where are all the good drivers? Driving in Upstate New York (Volume 2; nonfiction/education/awareness)

28) Risen from the Ashes: Broken Shackles, Part 2 (Volume 6; nonfiction/political awareness)

29) Risen from the Ashes: Broken Shackles, Two-Fer (Volume 7; nonfiction/political awareness)

30) A Twist in Travel: The Final Journey (science fiction/action; volume 4; end of series)

31) Risen from the Ashes: Identity Crisis (nonfiction; volume 8)

32) Risen from the Ashes: The First 8 (nonfiction; volume 9)

33) Risen from the Ashes: Imprisoning America (nonfiction; volume 10, end)

34) Challenge thy-self: Phase 1 (nonfiction; philosophy, self-help; volume 1)

35) Challenge thy-self: Phase 2 (nonfiction; philosophy, self-help; volume 2)

36) Challenge thy-self: Phase 3 (nonfiction; philosophy, self-help; volume 3)

37) Challenge thy-self: The complete Set (nonfiction; philosophy, self-help; All three phases combined)

38) CNY: Customer Awareness (nonfiction; reviews)

39) Avoiding Havoc (single Novel, fiction; Suspense, Thriller, Action;Coming soon)

40) Diabolical Excidious & Nyorloth (coming soon)

41) Toxic America: volume 1 (coming soon

bobby.simonds@gmail.com

www.facebook.com/bobbyraysimonds

www.facebook.com/bobbyrsimonds

www.instagram.com/@bobbysimonds

#bobbyraysimonds

#bobbysimonds

#BOBBYRAYSIMONDS

#ATWISTINTRAVEL

#risenfromtheashes

#toxicamerica

#Challengethyself